**STRUM IT GUITAR**

AUTHENTIC CHORDS
ORIGINAL KEYS
COMPLETE SONGS

# The Best of George Strait

## Contents

Arranged by Jeff Schofield

ISBN 978-0-634-01560-1

**HAL•LEONARD®**
CORPORATION

7777 W. BLUEMOUND RD. P.O. BOX 13819 MILWAUKEE, WI 53213

Visit Hal Leonard Online at
**www.halleonard.com**

# HOW TO USE THIS BOOK

*Strum It!*™ is the series designed especially to get you playing (and singing!) along with your favorite songs. The idea is simple—the songs are arranged using their original keys in *lead sheet* format, giving you the chords for each song, beginning to end. The melody and lyrics are also shown to help you keep your spot and sing along.

*Rhythm slashes* are written above the staff as an accompaniment suggestion. Strum the chords in the rhythm indicated. Use the chord diagrams found at the top of the first page of the arrangement for the appropriate chord voicings.

---

**Additional Musical Definitions**

| | |
|---|---|
| ⊓ | • Downstroke |
| ∨ | • Upstroke |
| **D.S. al Coda** | • Go back to the sign ( 𝄋 ), then play until the measure marked *"To Coda,"* then skip to the section labelled *"Coda."* |
| **D.C. al Fine** | • Go back to the beginning of the song and play until the measure marked *"Fine"* (end). |
| *cont. rhy. sim.* | • Continue using similar rhythm pattern. |
| N.C. | • Instrument is silent (drops out). |
| 𝄆 𝄇 | • Repeat measures between signs. |
| 1. 2. | • When a repeated section has different endings, play the first ending only the first time and the second ending only the second time. |

# Adalida

**Words and Music by Mike Geiger, Woody Mullis and Michael Huffman**

**Verse**

1. Oh ____ no, ____ here ____ you com-in' down the road. ____ With your cot-ton dress a-swish-in' you get-tin' some at-ten-tion from all ____ the boys in Thi-bo-daux. ____ Oh my, you real-ly fill-in' up their eyes. ____ Smil-in' and a-wink-in', I know what they think-in', but I'm the on-ly one who loves you so! ____

2. *See Additional Lyrics*

**Chorus**

A-da-li-da, pret-ty lit-tle ca-jun queen, ____ sweet ____ dix-ie flower, the belle ____

*Additional Lyrics*

2. Oh no, the hottest little dish I know.
   I know you can tell it;
   You're makin' me so jealous
   From my head down to my toes.
   Oh me, you could make a redneck green.
   The way that you're a-lookin',
   You got me a-cookin',
   And I ain't talking 'bout É toufee.

# All My Ex's Live in Texas

Words and Music by Lyndia J. Shafer and Sanger D. Shafer

*Additional Lyrics*

2. I remember that old Frio River
   Where I learned to swim.
   And it brings to mind another time
   Where I wore my welcome thin.
   By transcendental meditation
   I go there each night.
   But I always come back to myself
   Long before daylight.

# Carried Away

### Words and Music by Steve Bogard and Jeff Stevens

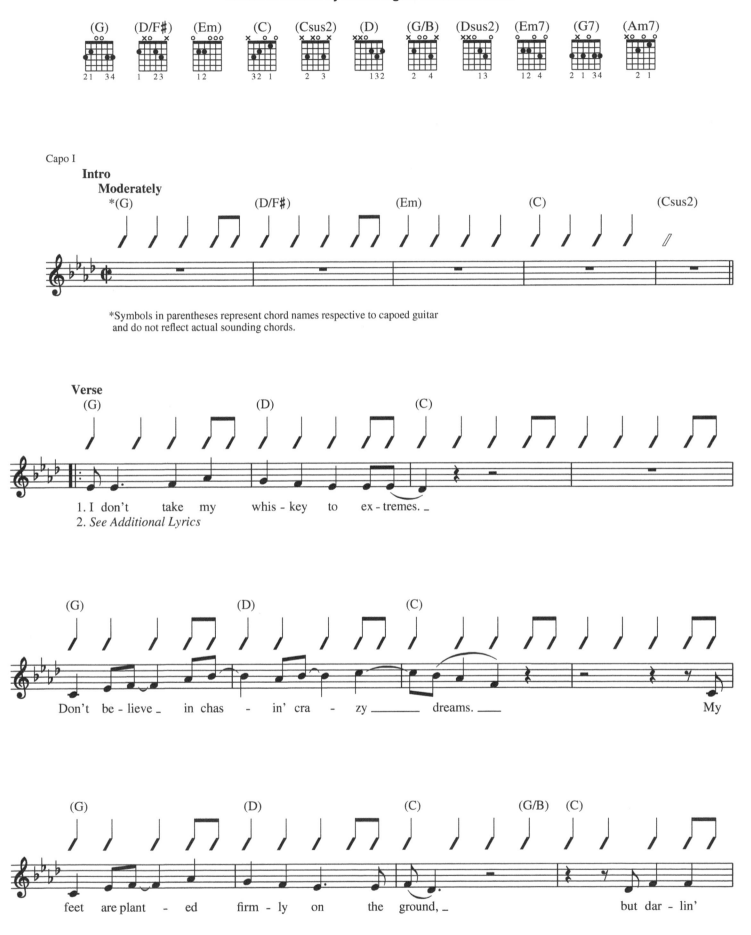

Capo I

**Intro**
**Moderately**

*Symbols in parentheses represent chord names respective to capoed guitar
and do not reflect actual sounding chords.

**Verse**

1. I don't take my whis - key to ex - tremes. _
2. *See Additional Lyrics*

Don't be - lieve _ in chas - in' cra - zy _____ dreams. _____ My

feet are plant - ed firm - ly on the ground, _ but dar - lin'

*Symbols in parentheses represent chord names respective to capoed guitar. Symbols above reflect actual sounding chords.

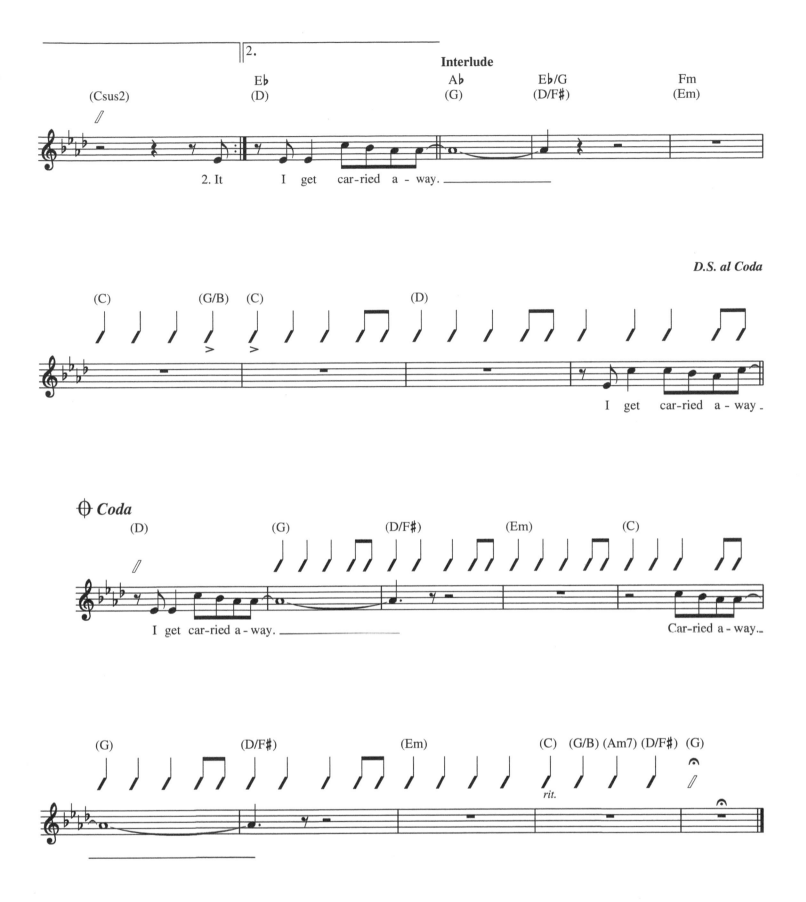

*Additional Lyrics*

2. It might seem like an ordinary night;
   Some ol' stars, the same ol' moon up high.
   But when I see you stand-in' at your door,
   Nothin's ordinary anymore.

# The Best Day

**Words and Music by Dean Dillon and Carson Chamberlain**

Capo II

**Intro**

**Moderately**

*Symbols in parentheses represent chord names respective to capoed guitar
and do not reflect actual sounding chords.

1. We

**Verse**

load - ed up __ my old __ sta - tion wag - on with a tent, a Cole - man and

2. *See Additional Lyrics*

sleep - in' bags, _____ some fish - in' poles, _ a cool - er of Cokes. _

**Symbols in parentheses represent chord names respective to capoed guitar.
Symbols above reflect actual sounding chords.

Three days be - fore we had __ to be back. When you're sev - en, you're in sev - enth heav -

- en when you're go - in' camp - in' in the wild __ out - doors. As we

turned off on __ that __ old __ dirt road, __ he looked at __ me __ and __ swore, __

**Chorus**

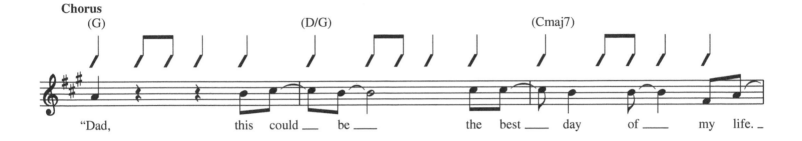

"Dad, this could __ be __ the best __ day of __ my life. __

__ I've been dream - in' day __ and night __ a - bout the fun { we'll __ / we've __

__ have. ____ } / __ had. ____ } Just me and you _____ do - in' what I've

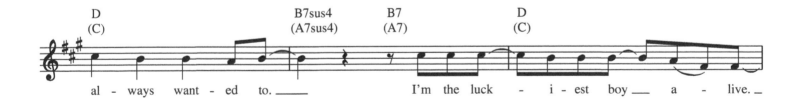

al - ways want - ed to. _____ I'm the luck - i - est boy __ a - live. __

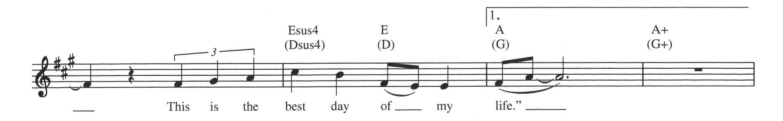

__ This is the best day of __ my life." _____

2. His life." _____

**Verse**

3. Stand-in' in a lit-tle room ___ back of the church ___ with our tux - es on, ___ look-in' at him ___ I say, ___ "I can't be - lieve, son, that you're grown." _____

**Chorus**

He said, "Dad, this could __ be __ the best __ __ day of __ my life. __ I've been dream - in' day __ and night __ of be-in' like __ __ you. _ And now it's me and her. _____ Watch-in' you __

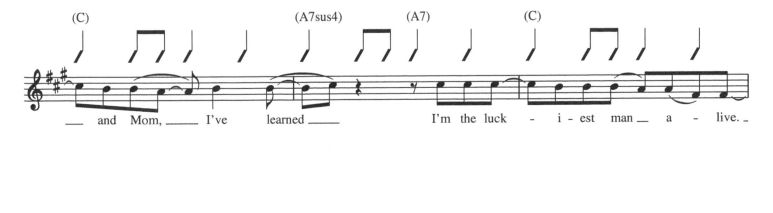

_____ and Mom, _____ I've learned _____ I'm the luck - i - est man _____ a - live. _

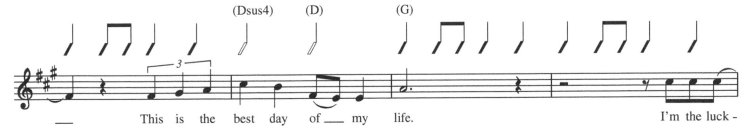

_____ This is the best day of _____ my life. I'm the luck -

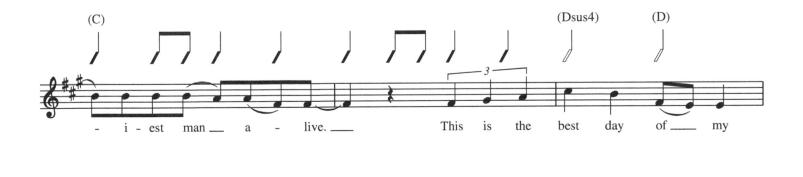

- i - est man _____ a - live. _____ This is the best day of _____ my

life." _____

*Additional Lyrics*

2. His fifteenth birthday rolled around,
   Classic cars were his thing.
   When I pulled in the drive with that old Vette,
   I thought that boy would go insane.
   When you're in your teens,
   Your dreams revolve around four spinnin' wheels.
   We worked nights on end till it was new again.
   And as he sat behind the wheel, he said, "Dad,...

# Blue Clear Sky

**Words and Music by Mark D. Sanders, Bob DiPiero and John Jarrard**

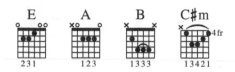

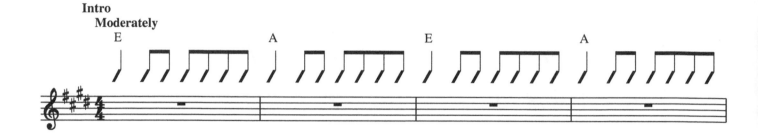

**Intro**
**Moderately**

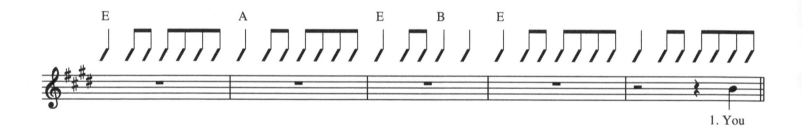

1. You

**Verse**

swear you've had e - nough. ___ You're read-y to ___ give up ___ on that

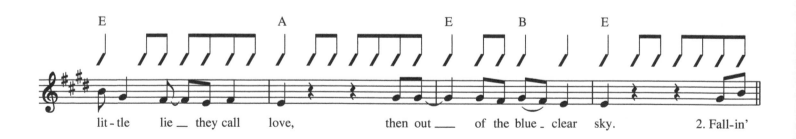

lit-tle lie ___ they call love, then out ___ of the blue ___ clear sky. 2. Fall-in'

**Verse**

right in - to ___ your hands ___ like rain on the de - sert sand, ___
3. *See Additional Lyrics*

___ it's the last thing you had planned, ___ then out ___

___ of the blue ___ clear sky.

**Chorus**

Here she comes, a walk - in' talk - in' true love, ___ say - in' I been

look - in' for you, love. ___ Sur - prise! ___ Your new ___ love ___ has ar - rived ___

out ___ of the blue clear sky. ___

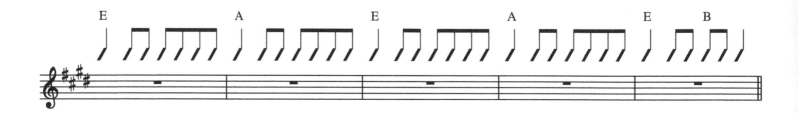

**Chorus**

Here she comes, a walk - in' talk - in' true love, __ say - in' I been look - in' for you, love. _____ Sur - prise! _ Your new __ love __ has ar - rived _____ _____ out _____ of the blue clear... Here she comes, a walk -

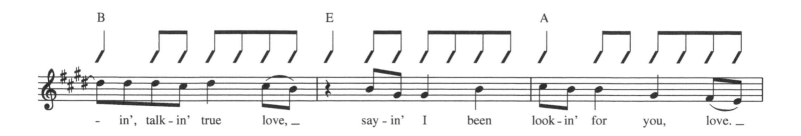

B                  E                  A

- in', talk-in' true    love, _    say-in' I been   look-in' for   you,    love. _

E                  B                  C#m

Sur - prise! _   Your new _ love _ has ar - rived _____ out _

A    B      E             A        B      E

_____ of the blue clear   sky, _        out _____ of the blue clear   sky. _

A                  E                  A                  E

*Additional Lyrics*

3. Ain't love a funny thing?
   One day you're givin' up the dream
   And the next you're pickin' out a ring
   Out of the blue clear sky.

# The Chair

**Words and Music by Hank Cochran and Dean Dillon**

Capo II

**Intro**
**Moderately Slow**

*Symbols in parentheses represent chord names respective to capoed guitar
and do not reflect actual sounding chords.

**Verse**

1. Well, ex - cuse ___ me, ___ but I think you've ___ got my ___

___ chair. No, that ___ one's not tak - en; I ___ don't mind if you ___ sit here. ___

**Symbols in parentheses represent chord names respective to capoed guitar.
Symbols above reflect actual sounding chords.

___ I'll ___ be ___ glad to share. __ Yeah, it's u - sually ___ packed ___

___ here on ___ Fri - day nights. ___ Oh, if you ___

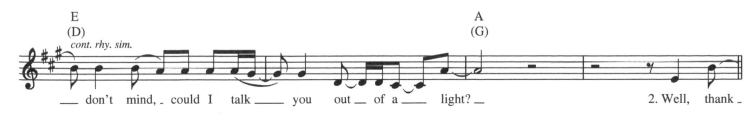

_cont. rhy. sim._

E (D) | A (G)

__ don't mind, __ could I talk __ you out __ of a __ light? __ 2. Well, thank __

**Verse**

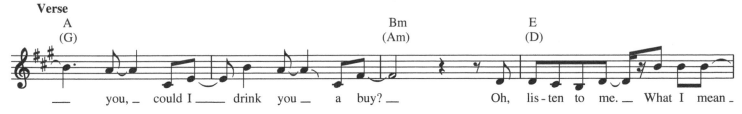

A (G) | Bm (Am) | E (D)

__ you, __ could I __ drink you __ a buy? __ Oh, lis-ten to me. __ What I mean __

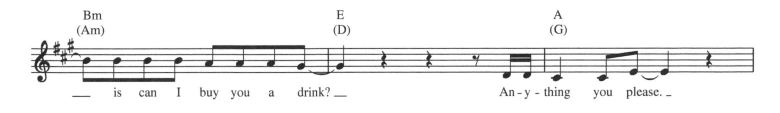

Bm (Am) | E (D) | A (G)

__ is can I buy you a drink? __ An-y-thing you please. __

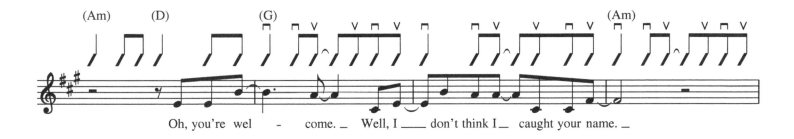

(Am) (D) (G) | (Am)

Oh, you're wel - come. __ Well, I __ don't think I __ caught your name. __

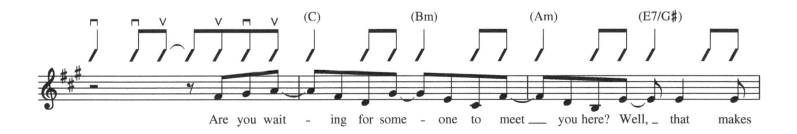

(C) (Bm) (Am) (E7/G♯)

Are you wait - ing for some - one to meet __ you here? Well, __ that makes

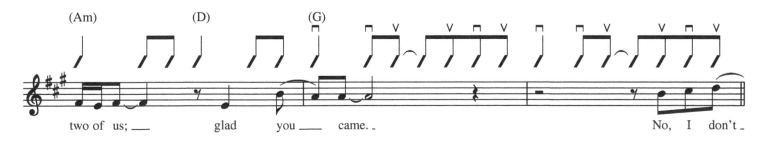

(Am) (D) (G)

two of us; __ glad you __ came. _ No, I don't __

**Chorus**

(Am) (D) (G)

__ know the name __ of the band, __ but they're good __ aren't __ they? Would you like to dance? __

Yeah, I like ___ the song too, ___ it re - minds ___ me of you ___ and me, ba -

- by. Do you think there's a chance ___ that ___ lat - er on ___ I could

drive you home? ___ No, I don't ___ mind ___ at ___ all. ___ Oh,

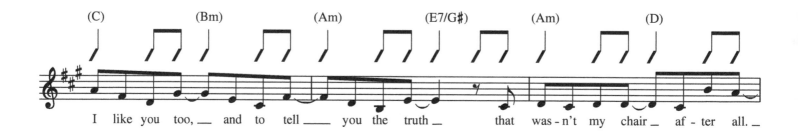

I like you too, ___ and to tell ___ you the truth ___ that was - n't my chair ___ af - ter all. ___

___ Oh, I like you too, ___ and to tell ___ you the truth ___ that

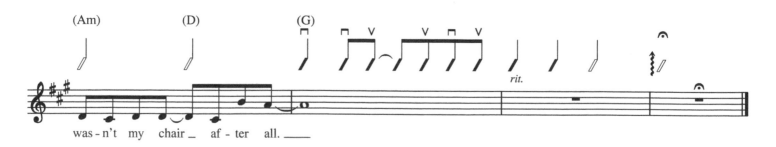

was - n't my chair ___ af - ter all. ___

# Does Fort Worth Ever Cross Your Mind

Words and Music by Darlene Shafer and Sanger D. Shafer

# I Can Still Make Cheyenne

Words and Music by Aaron Barker and Erv Woolsey

*Additional Lyrics*

2. He said it's cold out here and I'm all alone.
   Didn't make the short go again and I'm coming home.
   I know I've been away too long.
   I never got the chance to write or call
   And I know this rodeo has been hard on us all,
   But I'll be home soon and honey, is there somethin' wrong?

3. He left that phone danglin' off the hook,
   Then slowly turned around and gave it one last look.
   Then he just walked away.
   He aimed his truck toward that Wyoming line.
   With a little luck, he could still get there in time.
   And in that Cheyenne wind he could still hear her say…

# I Know She Still Loves Me

**Words and Music by Aaron Barker and Monty Holmes**

*Symbols in parentheses represent chord names respective to capoed guitar and do not reflect actual sounding chords.

**Symbols in parentheses represent chord names respective to capoed guitar. Symbols above reflect actual sounding chords.

*omit chord change, 2nd time          **see prior footnote

*Additional Lyrics*

2. She used to laugh at all my jokes,
   But lately I can't seem to make her smile.
   And the last time we made love
   It was good, but God, it's been a while.
   She's always there when I get home,
   But she's no longer waiting at the door.
   I know she still loves me,
   But I don't think she likes me anymore.

# It Ain't Cool to Be Crazy About You

**Words and Music by Dean Dillon and Royce Porter**

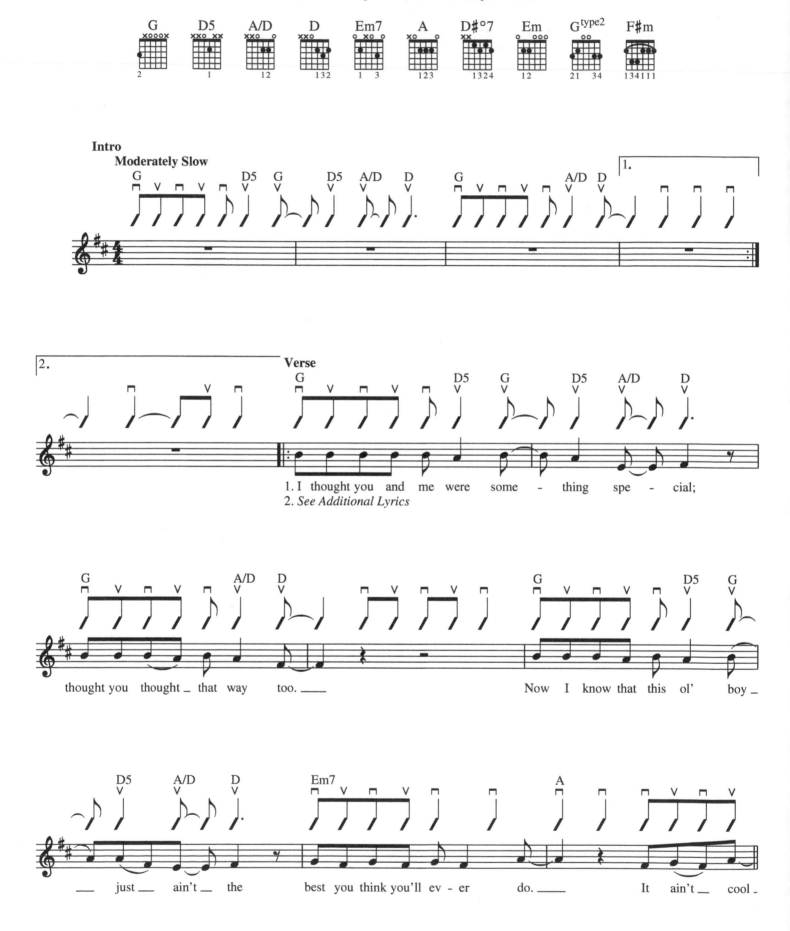

1. I thought you and me were some - thing spe - cial;
2. *See Additional Lyrics*

thought you thought _ that way too. ___ Now I know that this ol' boy _

___ just ___ ain't ___ the best you think you'll ev - er do. ___ It ain't ___ cool ___

*Additional Lyrics*

2. All of my friends they tried to tell me
   What and what not to do.
   It took a while for them to sell me but
   Finally they got through.

# Love Without End, Amen

**Words and Music by Aaron G. Barker**

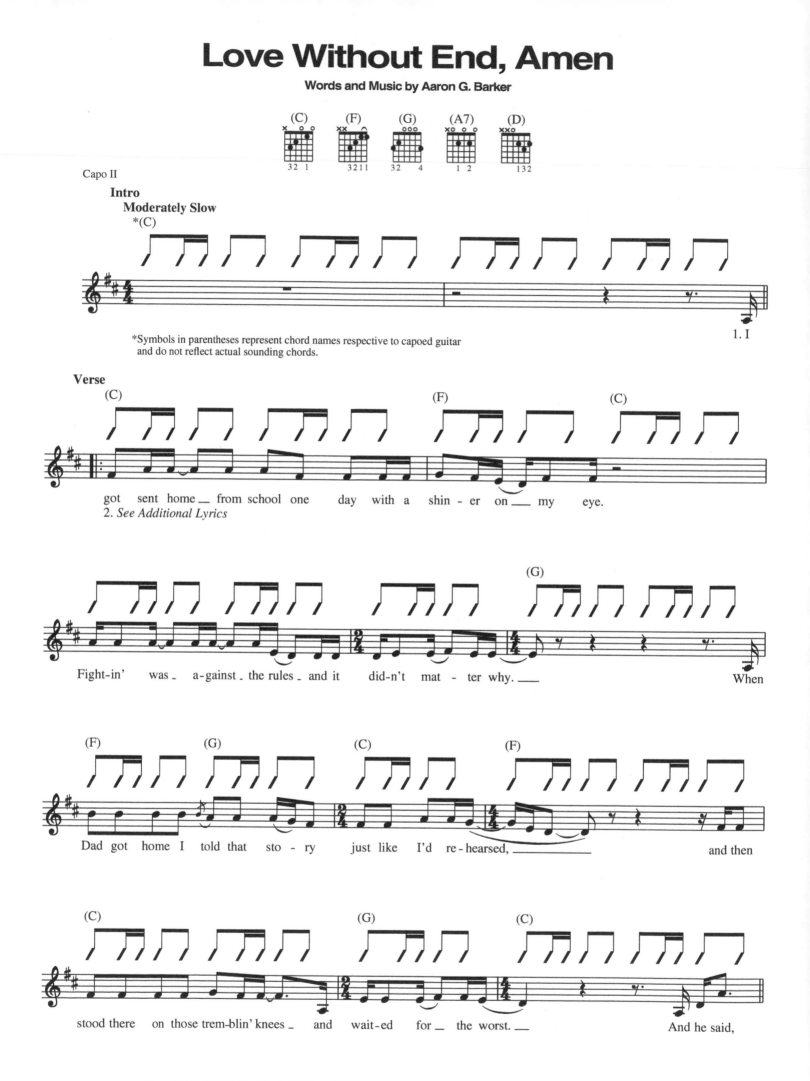

Capo II

**Intro**
**Moderately Slow**

*Symbols in parentheses represent chord names respective to capoed guitar and do not reflect actual sounding chords.

**Verse**

got sent home __ from school one day with a shin-er on __ my eye.
2. *See Additional Lyrics*

Fight-in' was __ a-gainst __ the rules __ and it did-n't mat-ter why. __ When

Dad got home I told that sto-ry just like I'd re-hearsed, __ and then

stood there on those trem-blin' knees __ and wait-ed for __ the worst. __ And he said,

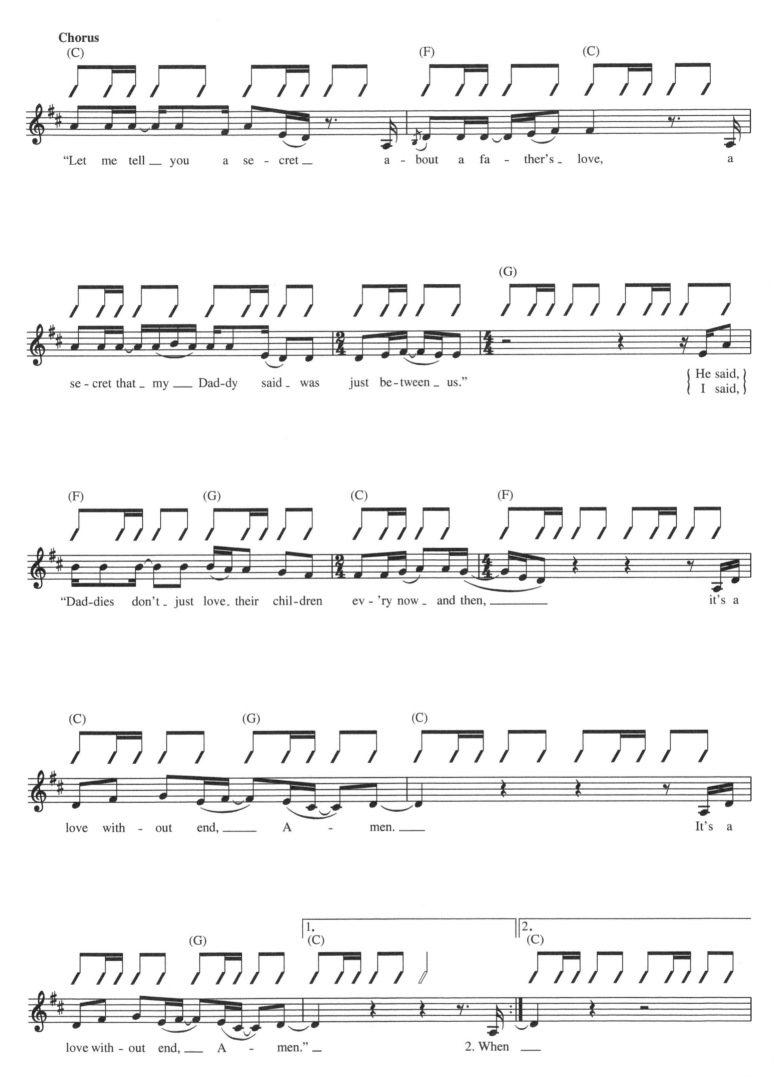

**Chorus**

"Let me tell _ you a se - cret _ a - bout a fa - ther's _ love, a

se - cret that _ my _ Dad-dy said _ was just be-tween _ us." He said, / I said,

"Dad-dies don't _ just love _ their chil-dren ev - 'ry now _ and then, _____ it's a

love with - out end, _____ A - men. _____ It's a

1. love with - out end, _ A - men." _   2. When _____

**Verse**

3. Last night I dreamed. I died. and stood out-side ____ those pearl-y gates.

When sud-den-ly, __ I re-al-ized __ there must be some __ mis-take.

If they know half the things __ I've done they'll

nev-er let __ me in. ____ And then some-where from the oth-er side I

**Chorus**

heard these words a-gain. ____ And they said, "Let me tell __ you a se-cret __ a-

bout __ a fa - ther's __ love, a se - cret that __ my ____ dad-dy said ____ was

just be-tween __ us." You see, dad-dies don't __ just love __ their chil - dren

ev - 'ry now __ and then, _____ it's a

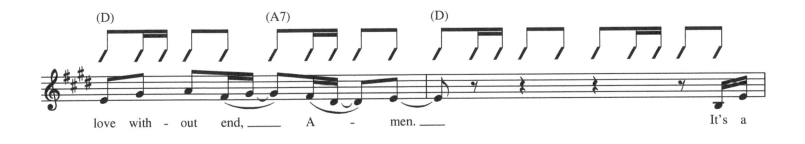

love with - out end, _____ A - men. _____ It's a

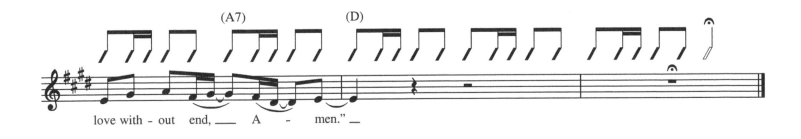

love with - out end, _____ A - men." ____

*Additional Lyrics*

2. When I became a father in the spring of eighty-one.
There was no doubt that stubborn boy was just like my father's son.
And when I thought my patience had been tested to the end,
I took my Daddy's secret and I passed it on to him.
I said…

# Lovebug

**Words and Music by Curtis Wayne and Wayne Kemp**

tried to out __ run it but it fin-'lly caught up __ with me. __ Tell me,

To Chorus

1.

how can I run from some - thin' that I __ can't see! __ Oh, that

2.

fooled me, hit me, real-ly took me by __ sur-prise. Oh, that

**Chorus**

lit-tle bit-ty teen-y ween-y thing they call the love bug. No-bod -

*cont. rhy. sim.*

- y's ev - er seen it, but it's got the whole __ world shook up.

It all start - ed with a lit-tle bit-ty kiss and a hug. It's a

*To Coda* ⊕

E             A

lit - tle bit - ty teen - y ween - y thing they call the love bug.

Interlude
A          E

            A

D         C# ⑤ 4fr D ④ open D# ④ 1fr

*D.S. al Coda*

E          A

2. Yeah, _ well, I

⊕ *Coda*

Chorus
A           E

Oh, that lit - tle bit - ty teen - y ween - y thing they call the love bug.

          A

No - bod - y's ev - er seen it, but it's got the whole _ world shook up.

*Additional Lyrics*

2. Yeah, well, I always thought that I had me a pretty good style,
But I lost that race by a good old country mile.
Yeah, I was walkin' all around with my head held way up high.
And it fooled me, hit me, really took me by surprise.

# The Man in Love With You

**Words and Music by Stephen Dorff and Gary Harju**

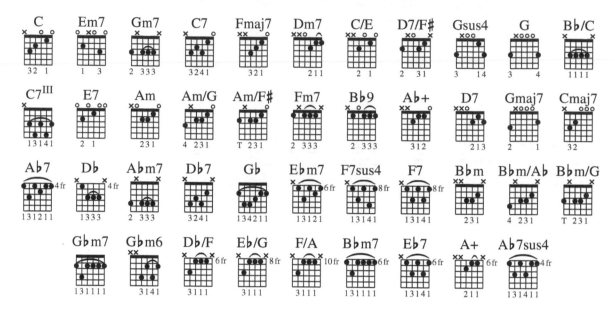

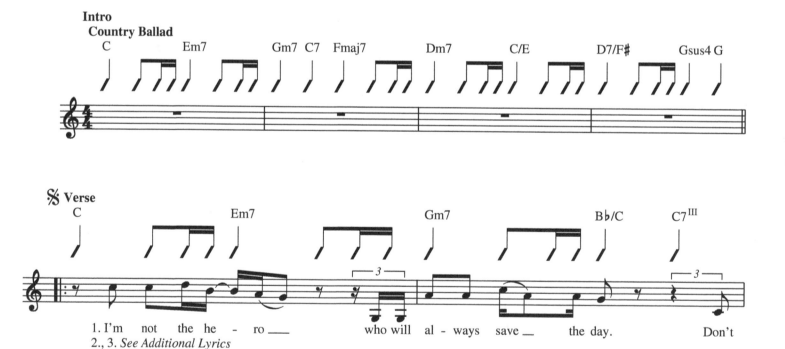

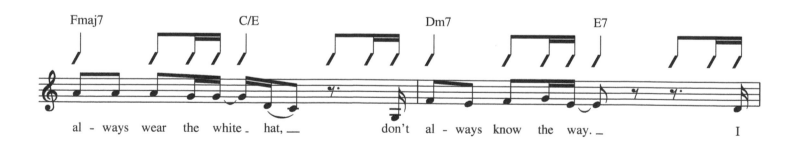

*Additional Lyrics*

2. I'm not the key that opens ev'ry door.
   I don't have the power to give you all you want and more.
   But when you're needin' somethin' special you can hold on to,
   I'll always be the man in love with you.

3. So when the world won't turn the way you wish it would
   And the dreams you have don't come alive as often as they should,
   Remember that there's someone there whose heart is always true.
   I'll always be the man in love with you.

# Ocean Front Property

**Words and Music by Hank Cochran, Royce Porter and Dean Dillon**

Lyrics:
1. If you leave __ me, I won't miss __ you and I won't ev-er take __ you back. __ Girl, your mem-'ry won't ev-er haunt __ me

2. *See Additional Lyrics*

'cause I don't love ___ you. ___ And now if you'll buy ___ that ___

**% Chorus**

I got some o - cean front prop - er - ty ___ in Ar - i -

zo - na. From my front - porch you can see the

sea. I got some o - cean front prop - er - ty ___ in Ar - i -

*To Coda*

zo - na. If you'll buy that ___ I'll throw the Gold - en Gate in

**1.**

**Interlude**

free. ___

D.S. al Coda

**Additional Lyrics**

2. I don't worship the ground you walk on.
   I never have and that's a fact.
   I won't follow or try to find you
   'Cause I don't love you.
   And now if you'll buy that…

# Right or Wrong

Lyric by Arthur Sizemore
Music by Haven Gillespie and Paul Biese

# One Night at a Time

**Words and Music by Roger Cook, Eddie Kilgallon and Earl Bud Lee**

*Additional Lyrics*

3. Tomorrow, well, that's another day.
   Come on, baby, now what do you say?
   Let's take our love one night at a time.

# Round About Way

**Words and Music by Steve Dean and Wil Nance**

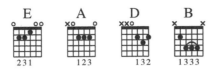

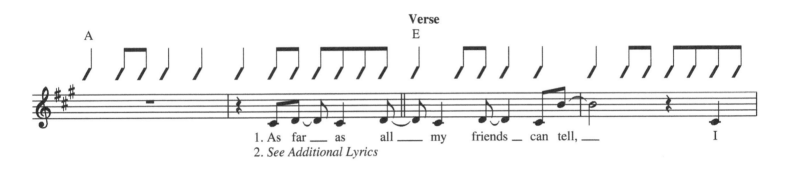

1. As far __ as all __ my friends __ can tell, __ I
2. *See Additional Lyrics*

took her leav - in' well. _____ That's kind - a right. __ 'Cause

when I'm out __ with them, __ I don't let __ her mem - 'ry

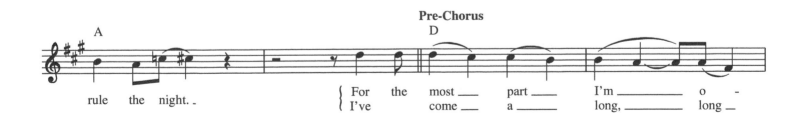

rule the night. __ { For the most __ part __ I'm __ o -
{ I've come __ a __ long, __ long __

in ____ a ____ round ____ a - bout _____ way. _____

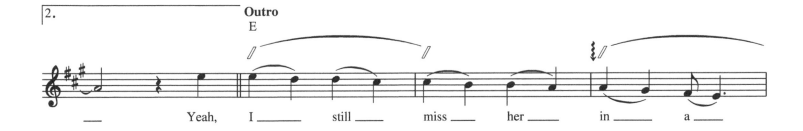

2. |_____| **Outro**

____ Yeah, I _____ still ____ miss ____ her _____ in _____ a _____

round __ a - bout _____ way. _____

*Additional Lyrics*

2. I no longer sit alone
For hours by the phone
Wishin' she would call.
And just the other day
I took her smilin' face
Down off my wall.

# We Really Shouldn't Be Doing This

### Words and Music by Jim Lauderdale

*Additional Lyrics*

2. Only an isolated incident,
But the acquaintance left me stunned.
The first attraction was the hardest hit
I thought I'd ever overcome.

*Chorus* 2. This kinda situation has to pass.
This chance encounter has to be the last;
To take it farther we would be remiss.
We really shouldn't be a-doin' this.

*Chorus* 3. We'd each be hurting somebody else
If we don't say our goodbyes real fast.
Won't even think about a farewell kiss.
We really shouldn't be doin' this.

# What Do You Say to That

**Words and Music by Jim Lauderdale and Melba Montgomery**

My heart knows this __ is real __ at last. _____ What do you say _____ to that?__

**Chorus**

Life _____ could nev - er be the same with-out you.

*cont. rhy. sim.*

Love __ was nev-er real-ly love with-out you. Here be - side you is real-ly where it's at. __

1.

What do you say __ to that? __

3. I

**Outro**

What do you say! __ You're like the warm __ sun - shine. ___ I

think of you all ___ the time. _____ I've fall - en for you __ and that's __

__ a fact. _____ What do you say _____ to that? ____

My heart knows this __ is real __ at last. _____ What do you say __ to that? __

*rit.*

*Additional Lyrics*

3. I promise I'll never leave.
   I'll always want you with me.
   Lovin' you won't never be old hat.
   What do you say to that?

# Write This Down

Words and Music by Dana Hunt and Kent Robbins

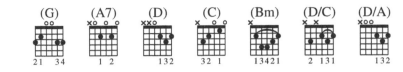

Capo I

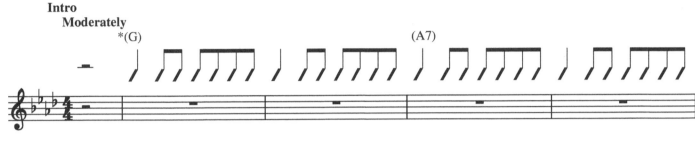

**Intro**
**Moderately**

*Symbols in parentheses represent chord names respective to capoed guitar
and do not reflect actual sounding chords.

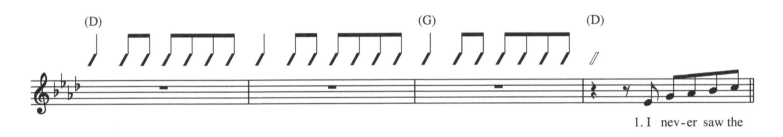

1. I nev-er saw the

**Verse**

end in ___ sight; ___ fools are kind of blind. ___

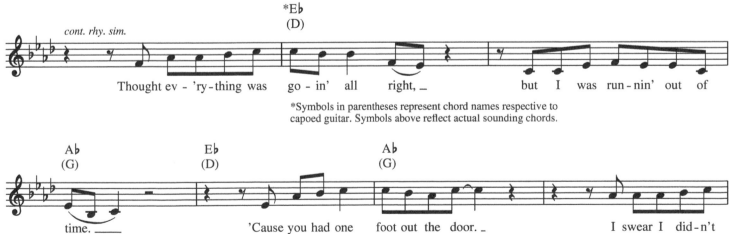

Thought ev - 'ry-thing was go - in' all right, ___ but I was run-nin' out of

*Symbols in parentheses represent chord names respective to
capoed guitar. Symbols above reflect actual sounding chords.

time. ___ 'Cause you had one foot out the door. _ I swear I did-n't

*Additional Lyrics*

2. I'll sign it at the bottom of the page.
   I'll swear under oath
   'Cause ev'ry single word is true
   And I think you need to know.
   So use it as a bookmark,
   Stick it on your 'fridgerator door,
   Hang it in a picture frame up above the
   Mantle where you'll see it for sure.

# AUTHENTIC CHORDS • ORIGINAL KEYS • COMPLETE SONGS

The *Strum It* series lets players strum the chords and sing along with their favorite hits. Each song has been selected because it can be played with regular open chords, barre chords, or other moveable chord types. Guitarists can simply play the rhythm, or play and sing along through the entire song. All songs are shown in their original keys complete with chords, strum patterns, melody and lyrics. Wherever possible, the chord voicings from the recorded versions are notated.

**THE BEACH BOYS' GREATEST HITS**
00699357............................... $12.95

**THE BEATLES FAVORITES**
00699249................................$15.99

**VERY BEST OF JOHNNY CASH**
00699514................................$14.99

**CELTIC GUITAR SONGBOOK**
00699265................................$12.99

**CHRISTMAS SONGS FOR GUITAR**
00699247................................$10.95

**CHRISTMAS SONGS WITH 3 CHORDS**
00699487.................................$9.99

**VERY BEST OF ERIC CLAPTON**
00699560................................$12.95

**JIM CROCE – CLASSIC HITS**
00699269................................$10.95

**DISNEY FAVORITES**
00699171................................$14.99

**MELISSA ETHERIDGE GREATEST HITS**
00699518................................$12.99

**FAVORITE SONGS WITH 3 CHORDS**
00699112................................$10.99

**FAVORITE SONGS WITH 4 CHORDS**
00699270.................................$8.95

**FIRESIDE SING-ALONG**
00699273................................$12.99

**FOLK FAVORITES**
00699517.................................$8.95

**THE GUITAR STRUMMERS' ROCK SONGBOOK**
00701678................................$14.99

**BEST OF WOODY GUTHRIE**
00699496................................$12.95

**JOHN HIATT COLLECTION**
00699398................................$17.99

**THE VERY BEST OF BOB MARLEY**
00699524................................$14.99

**A MERRY CHRISTMAS SONGBOOK**
00699211................................$10.99

**MORE FAVORITE SONGS WITH 3 CHORDS**
00699532.................................$9.99

**THE VERY BEST OF TOM PETTY**
00699336................................$15.99

**BEST OF GEORGE STRAIT**
00699235................................$16.99

**TAYLOR SWIFT FOR ACOUSTIC GUITAR**
00109717................................$16.99

**BEST OF HANK WILLIAMS JR.**
00699224................................$16.99

**HAL•LEONARD®**

Prices, contents & availability subject to change without notice.

Visit Hal Leonard online at
**www.halleonard.com**

0319
134